Original title:
Finding Myself Whole

Copyright © 2024 Swan Charm
All rights reserved.

Author: Sebastian Sarapuu
ISBN HARDBACK: 978-9916-89-622-8
ISBN PAPERBACK: 978-9916-89-623-5
ISBN EBOOK: 978-9916-89-624-2

Heartbeats of Self-Embrace

In the quiet whispers, I find my voice,
Each heartbeat a promise, a wondrous choice.
Embracing my shadows, with light from within,
In the dance of becoming, my journey begins.

The mirror reflects both scars and grace,
Each flaw a reminder of this sacred space.
In stillness I gather the strength of my soul,
In the warmth of acceptance, I discover my whole.

Every tear that I shed, a seed sown anew,
In the garden of healing, I flourish and grew.
With passion ignited, I boldly reclaim,
The canvas of life, I embrace without shame.

Love echoes softly, a melody sweet,
With each self-embrace, I rise to my feet.
The drum of my heart beats in perfect rhyme,
In the symphony of self, I transcend space and time.

So here I stand, a tapestry bright,
Woven with threads of my own inner light.
In the heartbeats of self, I find my way clear,
Through each pulse of compassion, my spirit is near.

An Odyssey of Self-Renewal

Beneath the vast sky, I embark on my quest,
To seek out the treasures that lie in my chest.
With each step I take, the horizon expands,
An odyssey forged by my own guiding hands.

The echoes of doubt whisper soft in my ear,
Yet courage ignites me; I silence the fear.
With visions of change weaving dreams into gold,
I embrace every story waiting to be told.

The seasons remind me of cycles and growth,
In the heart of the storm, I discover my oath.
For renewal resides in the ashes of pain,
Through trials and triumphs, I dance in the rain.

With fire in my spirit and peace in my mind,
I gather the pieces that once were confined.
Each fragment a gift, a lesson to heed,
In the garden of spirit, I plant my own seed.

The path may be winding, the night may be long,
Yet I find in each moment my heart sings its song.
An odyssey cherished, of self to unfold,
In the tapestry woven, my essence is gold.

Through valleys of silence, and mountains of light,
I rise with the dawn, renewed by the night.
In this journey of self, I embrace what is true,
An odyssey blossoming, forever anew.

The Heart's Hidden Atlas

In the quiet map of dreams,
Lies the path to distant stars.
Each heartbeat charts a course,
Through the seas of who we are.

Whispers guide the wandering,
In valleys deep and wide.
Finding solace in the night,
Where secret truths reside.

Footprints dance on memory's shore,
Tracing love through sands of time.
Every pulse a story told,
In rhythm and in rhyme.

Mountains rise and rivers flow,
Guiding hearts with gentle grace.
Through the storms and sunny days,
We navigate this sacred space.

Threads of fate we gently weave,
In patterns bold and bright.
The heart's atlas opens wide,
Revealing journeys in the light.

Reclaiming Lost Pieces

Once upon a canvas bare,
Colors faded, dreams untold.
In the shadows, fragments lie,
Waiting to be brave and bold.

Shattered mirrors, crooked frames,
Reflect the scars that linger still.
Gathering the scattered shards,
With every choice, we rise, we will.

Echoes of a distant laugh,
Resonate within the soul.
Rebuilding with each tender touch,
To reclaim and make us whole.

Hands outstretched to heal the past,
With gentle strokes of love and light.
Piecing together all we've lost,
To ignite the inner fight.

In the tapestry of time,
Each thread a story, rich and true.
Reclaiming all our lost pieces,
Creates a masterpiece anew.

Beneath the Shattered Surface

Underneath a fragile shell,
Lies a world of hidden grace.
Cracks and crevices unveil,
A beauty time can't erase.

Waves of sorrow ebb and flow,
Tides that wash the heart in pain.
Yet amidst the wreckage found,
Hope blooms like the softest rain.

Glimmers shine through brokenness,
Each fracture tells a vivid tale.
Lessons etched upon the heart,
As we rise despite the pale.

In the depths where shadows dwell,
Whispers of resilience grow.
Beneath the shattered surface,
Lies a strength we long to know.

Embracing all the shattered parts,
We craft a mosaic bright.
Beneath the cracks, a beating heart,
With courage that ignites the night.

Unfolding the Inner Tapestry

Threads of thought, both bold and fine,
Woven in the loom of time.
Each strand a memory, a dream,
In patterns intricate, sublime.

Colors dance and stories sing,
As we unfold the inner guide.
With each layer, truths emerge,
In the tapestry, we confide.

Silken whispers, tales of old,
Stitching moments, hearts entwined.
Through the needle's gentle eye,
We find the peace we seek, aligned.

Crafting joy amidst the pain,
With every knot and every tear.
In the artistry of our lives,
We create the love we share.

Unraveling the mystery,
Each thread a glimpse of grace.
In the unfolding tapestry,
We find our sacred place.

Spirit in Reflection

In quiet waters, whispers flow,
Mirrors reflect what hearts should know.
The soul lays bare, unmasked, unique,
In shadows deep, the truth we seek.

Each gaze reveals our hidden light,
A dance of thought in gentle night.
Threads of hope woven so tight,
In silent realms, we find our sight.

Voices echo in the still,
A soft reminder, a glowing thrill.
Through the dark, a spark ignites,
A guiding flame that warms our nights.

Embrace the silence, hear the sighs,
In the depths, no need for disguise.
The spirit speaks in calm refrain,
In stillness, we find joy and pain.

So let us linger, pause, and breathe,
In reflection's clasp, we shall weave.
A tapestry of what we are,
Infinite as the evening star.

The Canvas of Self-Discovery

A canvas blank, so wide and bright,
Awaiting strokes of pure delight.
Each splash of color tells a tale,
Where dreams are born and hopes set sail.

With every hue, the heart reveals,
Emotions deep that time conceals.
Brush in hand, we paint our fears,
Transforming pain to vibrant years.

In layers thick, our essence grows,
A wild mosaic of highs and lows.
Every brushstroke, a journey shared,
In artistry, our souls laid bare.

The palette speaks in silent tones,
Of laughter's song and sorrow's moans.
Each color blends, distinct yet whole,
A living testament of the soul.

So let us create with love and grace,
On this grand canvas, find our place.
In every stroke, a spark of bliss,
In self-discovery, we find our kiss.

Echoes of a Forgotten Dream

In twilight's hush, the memories play,
Echoes dance in soft array.
A dream once bright, now fades to gray,
Yet whispers linger, come what may.

Fragments linger in quiet nights,
Haunting shadows, flickering lights.
What once was clear now drifts away,
A fading song in disarray.

Yet in the stillness, sparks remain,
A pulse of hope through joy and pain.
In every sigh, a promise glows,
A thread of life that softly flows.

We chase the past with tender grace,
In each remembered dream, a trace.
Though time may blur the lines we drew,
The echoes remind us of what's true.

Embrace the dream, let it unfold,
In the heart's chambers, stories told.
For in the echoes of what's gone,
Lies the strength to carry on.

Paths of Reunion

In winding ways where souls converge,
A path unfolds, an ancient urge.
Footsteps echo, memories reign,
In the heart's embrace, love's refrain.

Each journey shared, a mark it leaves,
In bonds of trust, the spirit believes.
Through trials faced, we rise anew,
In the warmth of kinship, we break through.

The stars align in cosmic dance,
Destinies twine in sacred chance.
Across the miles, through time and space,
Our paths entwined, forever trace.

With every meeting, a story blooms,
A tapestry of light resumes.
In laughter and tears, we find our song,
In paths of reunion, we belong.

So let the journey, wide and free,
Guide all lost hearts back to sea.
For every step in love's embrace,
Is a step towards our destined place.

The Paradox of Self

In mirrors we find silent truths,
Reflections of what we wish to be.
A mask worn with a subtle grace,
Yet behind lies a deeper sea.

With every smile, a shadow shifts,
Two sides dance in brief embrace.
The heart yearns for a gentle light,
While doubts weave their tangled lace.

In solitude, we meet our fears,
A whisper lost in the loom of night.
But from the ashes, we emerge,
Stronger with each dawn's new light.

To find oneself in paradox,
Is to learn the art of being free.
Embrace the conflicting shades,
In this life's grand tapestry.

Beyond the Horizon of Me

I gaze afar, where dreams take flight,
The distant waves call out my name.
Through misty veils, I weave my thoughts,
Chasing whispers of soft acclaim.

Mountains rise with secrets old,
Each peak a story etched in stone.
Beyond the horizon, I seek truth,
In the silence of stars alone.

The sea reflects my wandering heart,
Its rhythm a song of endless plea.
The echoes of the past will guide,
As I step beyond the bends of me.

Fleeting moments drift like sand,
Each grain a piece of who we are.
In the vastness, we take our stand,
Finding wisdom in each scar.

The Anatomy of Peace

In quiet corners, harmony rests,
Soft whispers of a tranquil mind.
Threads of hope in a troubled world,
Weaving solace for hearts confined.

Through trials, patience learns to grow,
In every storm, a silver line.
The roots of peace entwine our souls,
In unity, we seek to shine.

With gentle hands, we mend the breaks,
In kindness, we find the healing grace.
For every wound, a balm exists,
In love's embrace, we find our place.

The anatomy of peace revealed,
In laughter shared and tears released.
We build a bridge with each kind word,
Together, rising, never ceased.

Celebrating the Unwritten

In blank pages, stories wait,
Whispers of dreams that yearn to thrive.
Every heartbeat holds a tale,
In silence, our aspirations dive.

Untold paths call for our feet,
Each moment, a chance to create.
With courage, we pen our own map,
Defining the ways we relate.

Beyond the lines of what we know,
Lies a canvas bright and wide.
In wild strokes, our joys unfold,
As we dance where hopes abide.

So raise a glass to inkless verses,
To futures not yet drawn in time.
In the blank space, we find our voice,
Celebrating what we will climb.

Portrait of a Journey

Winding paths beneath the sky,
Footprints whisper, passing by.
Mountains rise and valleys fall,
Every step begins a call.

The river flows with tales untold,
Stories woven, brave and bold.
Sunsets paint the evening's gold,
Hearts adventurous and old.

In the breeze, the memories dance,
Each heartbeat holds a chance.
Through the storms and sunny days,
Life unfolds in wondrous ways.

With every turn, a lesson learned,
In the fire, the spirit burned.
Traveling far and wandering wide,
In the journey, joy and pride.

At the end, reflections gleam,
Life, a vast and beautiful dream.
Every moment, a work of art,
A portrait painted from the heart.

The Blossoming Within

Silent seeds beneath the ground,
Whispers call, a gentle sound.
In the dark, potential waits,
Springing forth, it celebrates.

Petals open to the light,
Colors bloom, a pure delight.
Nature's grace in every hue,
Life awakens, fresh and new.

Roots entwined, a story sown,
In stillness, the strength has grown.
Facing storms, the blossoms sway,
Growing fiercely, come what may.

In their essence, courage sings,
Transformation, time it brings.
From within, the beauty thrives,
A testament that truth survives.

With gentle hands, the world can see,
The wondrous growth of you and me.
In every heart, a garden glows,
A symphony of love that flows.

Notes from the Inner Voyage

Sailing on a sea of dreams,
Navigating through the streams.
Stars above, a guiding light,
Charting courses through the night.

Every wave, a tale unfolds,
In the silence, wisdom holds.
Deep within, the echoes sound,
A treasure waiting to be found.

Seeking shores of self-discovery,
In the depths, it's you and me.
Exploring realms we cannot see,
Awakening our destiny.

Whispers carried on the breeze,
In the depths, the spirit sees.
Navigating hearts and minds,
In the journey, truth unwinds.

In the stillness, moments shine,
Painting landscapes, yours and mine.
In every heartbeat, a new song,
The inner voyage, where we belong.

Awakening the Silent Self

In the hush of early dawn,
A whisper wakes, the night is gone.
Shadows fade, the light breaks through,
In the silence, I find you.

Thoughts like petals, soft and dear,
Unfurling truths that persevere.
In each breath, a promise speaks,
In the quiet, the heart seeks.

Gentle echoes of the soul,
Leading to a deeper whole.
Awakening from tranquil dreams,
Filling life with sunlit beams.

In the mirror, reflections blend,
Transforming all that seems to end.
Each moment ripe with grace and breath,
A journey forward, beyond death.

Embracing all that I can be,
In the silence, I am free.
Awakening the silent self,
Finding joy beyond the shelf.

The Alchemy of Being

In the heart of night, we whisper dreams,
Where golden truths flow like silver streams.
Each moment a spark, a chance to see,
The hidden magic of simply being free.

The weight of doubts begins to fade,
In the warmth of light, shadows are laid.
Transform the pain, let love arise,
As we dance beneath the vast, open skies.

Fragments of hopes, like stardust, fuse,
In the quiet chaos, we choose to muse.
Elixirs of joy weave through the air,
A symphony echoes, everywhere.

Take a deep breath, let the moment unfold,
Molded by time, each story told.
With every heartbeat, we learn and grow,
In the alchemy of life, let our souls glow.

Together we rise, as one we stand,
Crafting our futures with gentle hands.
In the essence of now, we find our place,
The alchemy of being, a sacred grace.

When Shadows Come to Light

When the quiet falls, and darkness sighs,
Whispers of truth softly arise.
Under the stars, secrets untwine,
As shadows retreat, our spirits shine.

In the embrace of dawn's warm glow,
We unveil the fears we've come to know.
Facing the mirrors, our souls peep through,
In the light's embrace, we find what's true.

Moments of doubt, like clouds on the rise,
Fade in the brilliance of clear blue skies.
Courage awakens, fear starts to flee,
When shadows dissolve, we learn to see.

Gather the fragments, the light will mend,
Where pain had dwelt, let healing extend.
The journey unfolds like petals in bloom,
When shadows come close, they lead to room.

So here we stand, with hearts open wide,
Embracing the truth, we cannot hide.
Together we shine, with love as our guide,
When shadows come forth, there's nothing to bide.

Reflections in the Stillness

In the silence where thoughts converge,
Echoes of wisdom begin to surge.
Ripples of peace dance on the lake,
Reflections whisper, for stillness's sake.

Beneath the surface, a world unfolds,
Stories of joy, and tales of old.
In calm waters, we truly find,
The mirror of soul, the heart intertwined.

Time slows its march, a gentle grace,
In quiet moments, we see our place.
With open hearts, we search for light,
Reflections speak softly in the night.

Let go of noise, embrace the calm,
In stillness, we find a healing balm.
Each breath a story, a chance to be,
In reflections, we see our own decree.

Journey within, where peace may reside,
As thoughts drift away on the evening tide.
In the depths of silence, wisdom will flow,
In reflections of stillness, our true selves grow.

Notes from My Inner Journey

In the quiet of dawn, I pen my thoughts,
With ink of dreams and vibrant knots.
Each word a thread, connecting the soul,
Notes from within, making me whole.

Wandering paths of the heart's design,
Mapping the essence, both yours and mine.
Tracing the lines where shadows fall,
In the symphony of whispers, I hear the call.

Moments of doubt, like tangled vines,
In every struggle, the light aligns.
With each revelation, a truth is found,
Notes from the journey, a healing sound.

Embracing the storms, the calm that follows,
In the heart's embrace, new hope swallows.
Taking each step with intent and grace,
Notes from my journey, my sacred space.

So here I stand, pen in hand,
Writing my path in this vast, wide land.
With each stroke, I set my spirit free,
Notes from my inner journey, a melody.

Embracing the Fragmented

In shattered glass, reflections gleam,
Pieces of self in a fragile dream.
Each crack reveals a story bright,
Embracing fragments, finding light.

Scattered moments beneath the scars,
Whispers of hope in the midst of wars.
Holding close the jagged seams,
Crafting beauty from broken dreams.

Colors swirl in a chaotic dance,
Life's mosaic beckons a chance.
Through the fissures, love does seep,
In the cracks, the heart will leap.

Accepting fears, the unknown calls,
In the silence, the spirit stalls.
Yet, in the cracks, I find my way,
Embracing all, come what may.

With every shard, a lesson learned,
In the fragmented, eyes have turned.
A tapestry woven with strands so fine,
In the broken, I find the divine.

Tracing the Roots of Me

In the soil where shadows dwell,
Lies a tale time will tell.
Reaching down through earthen strands,
Tracing the roots with tender hands.

Whispers of ancestors softly sing,
Echoes of love that history brings.
Through winding paths, I seek the truth,
In the depths of my timeless youth.

Branches stretch towards the sky,
Yearning to soar, to reach up high.
Yet, within the heart, I find,
The strength of roots, forever bind.

Each leaf unfurls a fragile dream,
Tales of struggle, hope, and esteem.
Through tangled threads, I redefine,
In tracing roots, my heart aligns.

In the garden of what has been,
I gather courage from deep within.
Nurtured by love, grown from the past,
Tracing the roots, my spirit steadfast.

The Sanctuary of Solitude

In the quiet corners of my mind,
A sanctuary where peace I find.
Walls of silence, soft and deep,
In solitude, my soul can sleep.

Whispers of the heart take flight,
In stillness blooms the softest light.
Moments linger, a gentle pause,
Wrapped in stillness, my spirit draws.

Clouds drift softly across the sky,
I watch them roam, I let them fly.
Each thought a bird, free and clear,
In solitude, I hold them dear.

Time slows down, the world fades away,
In this refuge, I choose to stay.
Nature's breath, a soothing balm,
In this haven, I find my calm.

The sanctuary whispers gentle sighs,
Gathering hopes where stillness lies.
In every moment, I rediscover,
In solitude's arms, I find cover.

Unfolding the Hidden Garden

In the heart, a hidden place,
A garden waiting to embrace.
With petals curled, the secrets sleep,
In silent whispers, promises keep.

Sunlight dances through the leaves,
Awakening dreams that the heart believes.
Each bud unfolds with tender grace,
A journey unfolding, an endless space.

Roots entwined in the soil below,
Nurtured by love, by each gentle flow.
Every blossom tells a tale,
In the hidden garden, I set my sail.

Colors vibrant, scents collide,
In nature's arms, I choose to abide.
Through every storm, through every rain,
In the hidden, I find my gain.

As the seasons change and shift,
Unfolding layers, each a gift.
In the garden, I plant my dreams,
In whispers soft, the heart redeems.

The Quest for Inner Balance

In silence, whispers softly flow,
Through shadows where the stillness grows.
Each breath a step, a gentle guide,
To find the peace that lives inside.

The heart, a compass, beats so true,
With every choice, the self renews.
Amidst the chaos, seek the calm,
Embrace the storm; it brings the balm.

Beneath the surface, currents sway,
Yet in the depths, the light will play.
The journey bends but never breaks,
In fragments found, the spirit wakes.

A dance of shadow, light entwined,
The spirit's song, forever blind.
To find the balance, one must strive,
Within the chaos, love will thrive.

With open arms, the truth unfolds,
The quest for balance, stories told.
In every heartbeat, strength discerned,
The inner fire shall be returned.

Beneath the Veil of Reflection

A mirror holds a world so vast,
In stillness, whispers of the past.
Each glance reveals the soul's design,
A journey traced, both yours and mine.

In fragments deep, the shadows play,
Truth dances close, then slips away.
What hides beneath this fragile guise,
Are dreams awaiting our surprise.

The heart remembers every ache,
As memories weave and softly break.
Through tears, the light begins to shape,
The patterns of our own escape.

Awakening within, we learn,
To face the flames, to feel, to burn.
Beneath the veil, the spirit sings,
In every ending, hope takes wings.

With every glance, a deeper truth,
In timeless echoes, we are youth.
Beneath the veil, we find the key,
Unlocking love and unity.

Embers Igniting

In the stillness of the night,
Whispers kindled, sparks take flight.
Hope ignites in every heart,
A flicker's glow, a brand new start.

From ashes rise the dreams once lost,
Unyielding spirit, count the cost.
With every flame, the past will fade,
In radiant light, new paths are laid.

The warmth within can heal the cold,
In shared embraces, stories bold.
As embers dance, they weave the fate,
Of those who gather, hearts await.

In the darkness, light shall bloom,
Breaking through the heavy gloom.
A symphony of fire and air,
Creating magic everywhere.

So let the fire burn so bright,
In every moment, claim your right.
To be the spark, to shine your way,
Embers igniting, night to day.

Ceremonies of Self-Reconciliation

In solace, we unite as one,
Transforming grief to hope begun.
Each step, a ritual, a dance,
With open hearts, we take a chance.

In shadows cast by past mistakes,
We weave the threads, the heart remakes.
With every tear, a lesson learned,
In fires of truth, the spirit burned.

Gathering stories, both light and dark,
The pieces fit, no longer stark.
Each voice a part of crafted grace,
In unity, we find our place.

We honor paths that brought us here,
With every whisper, every fear.
Together we embrace the inner call,
In sacred moments, we stand tall.

Through ceremonies, hearts align,
Reconciliation, love defined.
With open arms, we heal the past,
In every moment, peace will last.

Fragments of a Silent Star

In twilight's hush, a spark does gleam,
Whispers of light in silent dream.
Shattered pieces of cosmic grace,
Floating softly in boundless space.

Each glimmer tells a story lost,
Chasing echoes at a heavy cost.
Fragments dance in the moonlit stream,
Kindling hope in each starlit beam.

They traverse through the velvet night,
Carving shadows, igniting bright.
Silent stories they long to share,
With souls adrift in the midnight air.

Invisible hands weave through the dark,
Stitching wishes with a glimmering spark.
An orchestra of light unfolds,
Tales of wonder forever told.

In the silence, they resonate,
Yearning for hearts that contemplate.
A silent star's flicker aligns,
Bringing solace through tangled lines.

The Journey to My Core

Upon quiet roads, I wander deep,
Searching where my secrets sleep.
Beneath the surface, truth resides,
A swirling tide where memory hides.

With every step, the ground gives way,
Whispers beckon, guiding my sway.
Voices echo from ages past,
Tales of shadows that gently cast.

I peel the layers, one by one,
Revealing glimpses of battles won.
In the heart of chaos, I find grace,
The shadows weave a warm embrace.

A lantern glows within the void,
Illuminating what once was shunned.
Every fear starts to dissolve,
In the warmth, my spirit evolves.

When I reach the core, I stand tall,
Embracing the truth beyond the wall.
For within the depths, I am restored,
A journey embraced, a soul adored.

Whispers of the Unseen

In the breeze, a secret glides,
Cloaked in whispers that nature hides.
With every rustle, stories flow,
From realms of shadows, soft and low.

Beneath the surface, worlds collide,
Voices flutter, secrets bide.
Cranes and crickets start to sing,
Echoing tales of forgotten spring.

Glimmers of truth hang in the air,
Unraveled gently, soft as prayer.
The unseen threads that bind us close,
Twisted in tales of joy and prose.

With every heartbeat, silence speaks,
Through hidden paths, the spirit seeks.
For in the stillness, I can hear,
The echoing whispers drawing near.

Embrace the quiet, heed the call,
Magic lingers, felt by all.
Open your heart, let whispers free,
To dance in realms of mystery.

Embracing the Mosaic

Each fragment shines in hues unique,
A patchwork quilt, the heart does seek.
Together woven, stories blend,
Creating beauty that has no end.

Colors splash in vibrant tones,
Healing pasts and tempered bones.
In every piece, a tale revealed,
A warm embrace, a wound concealed.

Assemble pieces, lost and found,
In the chaos, harmony is crowned.
A dance of laughter, tears, and dreams,
Crafting life's intricate seams.

With open arms, I welcome all,
Each voice a gem, no less, no small.
Together thriving, side by side,
A radiant world where hearts abide.

So here I stand, in this embrace,
A woven mosaic, a sacred space.
Through every crack, the light will pour,
Uniting us forevermore.

Moonlit Steps to Wholeness

Under a silver sky so bright,
I wander softly through the night.
Each step I take, the shadows blend,
In moonlight's glow, my spirit mend.

Whispers of dreams on the cool breeze,
A journey unfolds with such ease.
Through wooded paths and open fields,
The heart reveals what it conceals.

Stars twinkle like hopes above,
Guiding my steps, a gentle shove.
With every breath, I feel the flow,
A dance of light, my spirit grow.

As I embrace the night's sweet call,
I find my center, standing tall.
The moon's soft glow, a sacred friend,
In stillness, I know I'm transcending.

With each moonlit step, I unite,
Past and future in my sight.
A journey towards a radiant state,
In wholeness, I celebrate my fate.

The Roots of My Essence

In the soil of time, I grow deep,
Roots intertwined in memories I keep.
Whispers of ancestors echo near,
Their strength and wisdom in each tear.

Branches reaching for the sky,
In every challenge, I defiantly fly.
The storms may come, they bend, they sway,
Yet in my core, I stand and stay.

Each leaf a story, vibrant, alive,
In the garden of life, I strive.
Through seasons' change, I find my place,
Embracing my roots with a steadfast grace.

Nature's pulse within my veins,
Through joy and sorrow, love remains.
The essence of me, both strong and free,
In the roots of my being, I see me.

Nurtured by light, watered in time,
Each heartbeat echoes a silent rhyme.
From roots to blossoms, I ascend,
A story of life that will never end.

Finding Harmony in the Chaos

In swirling winds, the chaos brews,
Yet in my heart, a calmness hues.
Lost in the fray, I search for peace,
Amidst the noise, sweet moments cease.

Notes of laughter pierce the dark,
Guiding my soul like a gentle spark.
Through tangled paths, I seek the light,
Finding my rhythm, igniting the fight.

A symphony plays in the midst of strife,
Melodies woven through the fabric of life.
In every discord, a lesson is learned,
Through trials faced, my spirit has turned.

With each heartbeat, the chaos sings,
Transforming struggles into beautiful things.
Embracing the mess, I dance and sway,
Finding my harmony, come what may.

In the storm's eye, I stand with grace,
Breathing in chaos, I'm finding my place.
With open arms, I welcome the wave,
In the dance of life, I am brave.

A Symphony of Solitude

In quiet moments, music plays,
Soft and subtle, in gentle ways.
A symphony born from silence deep,
In solitude's arms, my spirit leaps.

Each note a whisper, soft and clear,
Echoing dreams I hold so dear.
Alone, yet not lonely, I find my bliss,
In stillness, the world I gently kiss.

Time stretches out like a warm embrace,
In solitude, I find my place.
Melodies twirl in the evening air,
A dance of thoughts, beyond compare.

With every heartbeat, harmonies swell,
In the depths of calm, I hear the bell.
Calling me forth to explore my soul,
In solitude's grip, I become whole.

So here I stand, in reverie's glow,
A symphony of self, in a tender flow.
Through solitude, I learn to see,
The beauty of being, simply me.

The Rhythm of Inner Light

In silence, whispers dance so bright,
A melody of dreams takes flight.
Each heartbeat echoes with pure delight,
Guiding us through the endless night.

Stars align in a story told,
In the tapestry of the bold.
With every step, we dare to unfold,
Our souls ignite, a light uncontrolled.

We sway to the pulse, the inner song,
Finding where we truly belong.
In the cosmic flow, we grow strong,
Together we rise, where we once were wrong.

With every breath, we touch the divine,
In the rhythm of love, we intertwine.
With grace and hope, our spirits shine,
In the dance of life, we align.

Through shadows cast, we see the glow,
Each lesson learned, a chance to grow.
In the embrace of peace, we sow,
The seeds of light, in hearts we know.

Cultivating Inner Wholeness

In fragile hands, we hold our dreams,
Nurturing hope within our seams.
With gentle hearts, we weave our beams,
Creating strength from silent screams.

Through the cracks, the light does pour,
Revealing paths to self and more.
In the garden of our inner core,
We blossom forth, forever soar.

With every tear, a seed is sown,
In the soil of love, we've grown.
In the quietude, we're never alone,
Finding the wholeness we have known.

Embracing flaws, we learn to bend,
In our brokenness, we find a friend.
As we journey, the curves extend,
To wholeness where our hearts can mend.

In the mirror, a reflection true,
Of the journey and all we pursue.
With open arms, we welcome the view,
Cultivating love in all we do.

The Journey to Inner Freedom

In the depths of night, we seek the key,
Unlocking chains to let us be free.
Through shadows deep, we learn to see,
The light within, our sanctuary.

With every step, we shed the past,
Like petals falling, a gentle cast.
In the stillness, we find at last,
A heart unbound, our spirits vast.

The road may twist, the path may turn,
In the furnace of life, we learn.
Through trials faced, a fire we burn,
For in each struggle, we discern.

As wings take flight, we rise above,
In the embrace of a deeper love.
With courage found, we fit like a glove,
In the dance of life, we move and shove.

Finding solace in our own skin,
Embracing freedom's song within.
With open hearts, we dare to begin,
The journey of life, where we all win.

Embracing the Unfolding Path

In every step, a story is spun,
Under the moon, beneath the sun.
With open arms, we welcome the fun,
Embracing life's dance, we've just begun.

Each twist and turn, a lesson learned,
In the fire of life, we blaze and burned.
With every heartbeat, our passions churned,
On the path ahead, our souls returned.

With courage felt, we face the unknown,
In the garden where seeds are sown.
With every breath, our essence grown,
In the winds of change, we find our own.

Together we journey, hand in hand,
As we traverse this sacred land.
With dreams laid forth, futures planned,
In the embrace of life, we stand.

With joy we celebrate the ride,
In the unfolding, no need to hide.
With love as our compass, we abide,
In the dance of existence, side by side.

The Canvas of Self

Each stroke reflects a quiet thought,
Colors blend in battles fought.
A palette rich with hopes and dreams,
Awakening what sunlight seems.

Whispers paint the corners bright,
Shadows dance in soft twilight.
Identity, a work in progress,
A masterpiece of truth, no less.

Every blemish tells a tale,
Of valleys deep and winds that wail.
Layer upon layer, brave and bold,
Stories etched in hues of gold.

As time drips, the canvas grows,
A tapestry that ebbs and flows.
Reflections change with every glance,
In every shade, a hidden chance.

And when the masterpiece is done,
A journey shared, a life won.
In each color, love and strife,
The canvas holds the pulse of life.

Echoes of Authenticity

Voices rise from deep within,
Truth be told, where all begins.
An echo of the heart's own beat,
In silence, souls dare to meet.

Beneath the noise, a whisper stirs,
Reminding us of who we were.
Authentic paths are seldom straight,
Each twist reveals a brand new fate.

Eyes that shine with stories bright,
Glancing back through shades of light.
Carved from dreams that dared to soar,
They echo truths, forevermore.

With every choice, a step we take,
Each voice a ripple in the wake.
In unity, our tales unfold,
Together, treasures yet untold.

Resonate with every breath,
In authenticity, find your depth.
Let echoes guide and shape your way,
In every dawn, embrace the day.

The Alchemy of Identity

In a crucible of longing hearts,
Elements dance, chemistry starts.
Mixing hopes with strands of fate,
Alchemy transforms, it's never late.

With every change, a formula binds,
Crafting truths that life reminds.
What once was lead, now turns to gold,
Identity, a story told.

In the furnace of trials and tears,
Emerging strong through whispered fears.
Elixirs brewed from pain and joy,
Sculpting self, a timeless ploy.

The potion swirls with every breath,
Merging life, love, and even death.
Transmuting sorrow into light,
Identity, a wondrous sight.

And in this dance of dark and bright,
We find ourselves, ignite the night.
An alchemist at heart, we'll be,
Creating magic, wild and free.

Beneath the Layers

Peeling back the skin of years,
What lies beneath? Joy or fears?
Every layer, a hidden story,
Fragments of past, pain, and glory.

Brush away the dust of doubt,
Reveal the truth that seeks to shout.
Beneath the layers, love resides,
An ember glowing, deep inside.

Worn-out fabric, torn yet strong,
Threads of self in every song.
A pattern formed from scars and grace,
Testaments of life's embrace.

Each unraveling unveils the whole,
A mosaic pieced with every soul.
What we wear is not the truth,
Beneath the layers lies the proof.

So dare to delve, explore the deep,
In every heart, a secret keep.
Uncover love, let shadows fade,
Beneath the layers, dreams are made.

Navigating the Labyrinth

Twisting paths beneath dim light,
Whispers echo in the night.
Shadows dance and play their game,
Lost within, yet seeking fame.

Steps can falter, heart can race,
Trusting instincts in this space.
Every turn a chance to grow,
Finding strength in what we know.

Walls that confine can soon reveal,
Lessons learned to help us heal.
Caught in cycles, we ascend,
Navigating till the end.

Threads of hope weave through the dark,
Guiding us to find the spark.
Though the maze is vast and wide,
In our hearts, the truth will bide.

Emerging from this twisted quest,
With a heart that feels the best.
Navigating through the fear,
A brighter path now drawing near.

The Fusion of Disparate Dreams

Colors blend and shadows fade,
In this dance, the dreams are made.
Visions flicker in the night,
That entwine with boundless light.

Fragmented hopes, a puzzle's piece,
Synthesis brings sweet release.
Harmony in chaos found,
In the silence, love's profound.

Crossed paths of fate intertwine,
Different stories now align.
Merging thoughts on whispered winds,
Where every journey truly begins.

Weaving threads of varied hues,
Creating worlds, new and true.
In the tapestry of dreams,
Unity in all it seems.

Letting go to find the whole,
Embracing depth within the soul.
The fusion glows, unbound it gleams,
This adventure built from dreams.

Rebuilding the Heart's Architecture

Cracks and creaks in fragile walls,
Echoes of past emotional calls.
Within the ruins, hope takes flight,
Designing love through the night.

Blueprints sketched with careful hands,
Framing dreams on shifting sands.
Every beam a tale untold,
Structure built on courage bold.

Windows open to the sky,
Letting light in, fears awry.
Foundation strong, the heart will stand,
Reimagining with a steady hand.

With each brick, a memory laid,
In the colors, joy displayed.
Restoration in every heart's beat,
Building spaces that feel complete.

Patience nurtures what we build,
Forgiveness flows, the heart is filled.
In this craft, we find our way,
Rebuilding love, day by day.

A Star Amongst the Ashes

In the remnants of the past,
Flickers shine, they hold steadfast.
Broken dreams, like ashes strewn,
Yet a spark can break the gloom.

Out of dark, a glow appears,
Whispering through hidden fears.
Every wish that seemed to die,
Rises gently, learns to fly.

Through the night, the star will gleam,
Lighting paths, igniting dreams.
Born from loss, yet fierce and bright,
In the dark, a hopeful light.

Lessons learned through fire's test,
Show us how to truly rest.
Amongst the ruins, beauty found,
A star whispers, joy unbound.

So let the ashes softly fade,
As the light begins its parade.
From the chaos, we will rise,
Finding strength beneath the skies.

A Quest for Lost Whispers

In the forest, shadows sigh,
Echoes of dreams passing by.
Footsteps on a winding trail,
Guided by stories, pale and frail.

Stars flicker in the night's embrace,
Whispers of time leave their trace.
Each moment a delicate thread,
Tales of the living and the dead.

Through the mist, a lantern glows,
Illuminating what one knows.
In silence, secrets softly bloom,
Filling the heart with muted gloom.

A quest for echoes long since lost,
Navigating through dreams that cost.
Every heartbeat a step to take,
In these shadows, it's truth we make.

With every whisper, wisdom sings,
Nature's hand, the soul it brings.
Chasing phantoms, daring flight,
Seeking warmth in the cold night.

The Embroidery of Experience

Threads entwined in life's vast loom,
Colorful tales of joy and gloom.
Each stitch a memory, finely sewn,
Crafting the fabric we've all known.

Patterns shifting with every tear,
Restitch the seams with love and care.
Golden moments, silver strife,
Weaving together the tapestry of life.

In shadows dance the threads of fate,
Frayed edges tell stories, we create.
We lug our burdens, hopes held tight,
In this embroidery of light and night.

Each knot a lesson, every hue
Paints the story of me and you.
Through laughter's joy and sorrow's sting,
In every corner, memories cling.

The fabric shifts as seasons change,
New threads emerge, feeling strange.
But in this weave, we find our place,
The tapestry of the human race.

Threads Woven in Solitude

In quiet corners, thoughts unwind,
A tapestry of the heart, confined.
Each thread a whisper, soft and light,
Woven in shadows, out of sight.

The loom of silence stretches wide,
Where dreams and fears do often hide.
Frayed edges speak of wars within,
Battles fought where few have been.

Emotions linger, delicate strands,
Crafted in solitude's quiet hands.
Through solitude, we find our way,
Threads intertwining in shades of gray.

With every stitch, a story breathes,
Patterns shifting like fallen leaves.
In silence, beauty starts to grow,
As we wander where few dare go.

Eclipsed in quiet, we employ,
Solitude's hand, we're learning joy.
In woven tales, we find our truth,
In solitude's embrace, eternal youth.

Through the Mirror of Time

Reflections ripple across the glass,
Moments trapped as they swiftly pass.
A glance reveals what once was real,
In the mirror, our fate we feel.

Time distorts the lines of past,
Memories linger, shadows cast.
Whispers echo from distant shores,
In the depths, the soul explores.

Through corridors of what has been,
Woven in light, stitched with sin.
Every heartbeat a ticking clock,
Facing the past with every shock.

Visions flicker in muted hues,
Painting a world of vibrant blues.
In this glass, our stories twine,
Love and loss through the sands of time.

Yet in this mirror, hope remains,
A glimmer through the joy and pains.
Embrace the journey, let it guide,
Through the looking glass, we stride.

Shards of My Soul's Mirror

Fragments glimmer in the dark,
Reflecting dreams lost to time.
Within each piece lies a spark,
A whisper of my heart's chime.

Shattered edges tell a tale,
Of courage in each broken part.
Though weary, I shall not fail,
To gather strength from my heart.

In the silence, I will mend,
Each shard a lesson to embrace.
In the depths, I find a friend,
Resilience shines on my face.

I'll stitch the echoes of my past,
With threads of hope and woven dreams.
A tapestry that will hold fast,
Illuminating what life deems.

And when I rise from these remains,
A new reflection I will see.
In every scar where beauty reigns,
The mirror shows the soul in me.

The Resurgence of Forgotten Light

In the depths of fading night,
A flicker stirs beneath the gray.
Whispers gently call the bright,
To bring the dawn, to light the way.

Shadows tremble, old and cold,
As warmth breaks free from its cage.
Stories of the brave retold,
With spirits fierce and hearts ablaze.

Lost reveries begin to soar,
With memories that time forgot.
A luminous tale from yore,
Resurrecting all that was wrought.

In every heart, a spark resides,
Anticipating the dawn's sweet rise.
Nature's breath, the moon abides,
As stars compose their lullabies.

So I stand before the morn,
Embracing shadows left behind.
In every loss, a light is born,
A journey to the truth defined.

In the Embrace of Wholeness

In stillness, I find my core,
Each fragment dances in the light.
With open arms, I explore,
The beauty of the day and night.

Unity in all I see,
Every piece a vital part.
In the depths, I find the key,
To unlock the sacred heart.

Harmony in every breath,
Echoes of the universe.
In the fear of life and death,
I embrace the wondrous curse.

Merging shadows with the sun,
In the chaos, I can thrive.
Every journey can be fun,
When I choose to feel alive.

In the web of life's design,
Each thread connects us with grace.
In the embrace, I am divine,
A tapestry of time and space.

The Dance of the Unbroken

In the rhythm of the night,
Bodies sway beneath the stars.
Every heart beats bold and bright,
Freed from the weight of their scars.

With each twirl, the echoes sing,
A sonnet of the brave and free.
In this moment, we take wing,
Dancing to our melody.

Fingers intertwined as one,
We surrender to the flow.
Embracing shadows, basking sun,
In every step, our spirits grow.

The music carries us afar,
Revealing secrets of the night.
With every glance, we raise the bar,
Reflecting pure and timeless light.

Let the world fade, let it cease,
As we whirl in our delight.
In this dance, we find our peace,
Together, we are unbroken, right.

The Bridge of Self-Understanding

On the edge of thought, I stand,
Gazing deep into my mind.
Each whisper offers a guiding hand,
Through shadows, truth I find.

With every step, I shed the past,
Revealing layers once concealed.
In the stillness, lessons amassed,
My heart, again, is healed.

Mirrors of doubt fade from sight,
As courage fills the air.
The bridge stands tall in fading light,
Showing me it's time to care.

In every crack, a story flows,
Of battles fought, of bright tomorrows.
I walk with grace, as wisdom grows,
Embracing joy, releasing sorrows.

Self-understanding lights the way,
As I journey toward the dawn.
Forging strength from yesterday,
The bridge, my spirit's song.

Awash in Solitary Reflections

In quiet depths, the echoes call,
Whispers dance upon the breeze.
Each moment drifts, a gentle fall,
Awash in contemplative ease.

Beneath the stars, I find my peace,
In solitude's warm embrace.
Thoughts unwind, my mind's release,
Time slows in this sacred space.

Ripples on a silent lake,
Carry stories not yet told.
In solitude, the heart will wake,
To truths both gentle and bold.

With every sigh, I forge a bond,
With shadows that cradle my soul.
Reflections shape the path to wander,
Revealing me, my spirit whole.

Awash in solitude, I tread,
Where clarity's light softly shines.
Each thought, a thread once more spread,
In the tapestry of the mind.

Chronicles of a Reclaimed Soul

Pages turn in windswept days,
Tales of heartache, joy, and strife.
In every line, a flicker stays,
Of moments lived, a vibrant life.

Once adrift in storms of doubt,
I searched for shores, a guiding light.
Now, with strength, I stand, no doubt,
A reclaimed soul ready for flight.

Ink runs deep, the story flows,
As past and present intertwine.
With every breath, new wisdom grows,
The future's bright, my heart aligns.

With open arms, I greet the dawn,
No burden left, just hope remains.
Each chapter sung, no longer gone,
A testament to love's refrains.

Chronicles filled with laughter's sound,
In every heart, a journey starts.
In turned pages, hope is found,
Reclaimed, my soul, forever imparts.

The Language of the Heart

In silence, words are born anew,
A dialect of soul and art.
Each heartbeat sings, both loud and true,
A symphony of life's pure heart.

Through gentle gaze, a story told,
Embracing all that we can be.
In warmth and love, we break the mold,
Unraveling deep, the mystery.

With every touch, connection grows,
A language that transcends the lies.
In presence felt, the spirit knows,
No need for words, just truth that flies.

Listen close, the whispers say,
In every pulse, the world's embrace.
The language of the heart will stay,
In timeless dance, we find our place.

Together we weave our tale so bright,
As hearts unite, we spread our wings.
In love's embrace, we shine our light,
Creating joy in all our beings.

In Search of Lost Echoes

In twilight's embrace, whispers linger,
Memories drift like leaves in the wind.
Footsteps retrace the paths of old,
Seeking the echoes time has pinned.

Beneath the boughs where shadows dance,
The heart recalls a gentle sigh.
Fragments entwined, a fleeting glance,
Chasing the laughter that waved goodbye.

Each murmur speaks of tales untold,
Woven in dreams that seldom weave.
The scent of jasmine, a story sold,
In the garden where I grieve.

Through silent halls and crumbling stone,
The ghost of joy calls out in vain.
I wander where the light has shone,
Searching for echoes in the rain.

Yet amidst the fog, a spark ignites,
Hope unfurling, a fragile thread.
In darkened corners, the heart still fights,
For lost echoes that dance like the dead.

Pieces of a Forgotten Dream

Scattered petals on an old pathway,
Whispers of wishes never claimed.
Each fragment holds a tale to say,
Of nights lit by stars, unashamed.

A canvas torn, colors that fade,
Moments linger like dust in the air.
Shadows stretch where memories played,
Dreams entwined in a silent prayer.

Once vibrant hues, now shades of gray,
Echoes of laughter, a fleeting spark.
In fragile hearts, the hopes still stay,
Hiding within, deep in the dark.

With every breath, a wish unspools,
Threads of longing, gently sewn.
In the quiet realm, time rewrites rules,
Crafting a place we can call home.

As dawn breaks softly, shadows recede,
Pieces of dreams find a way to blend.
In the heart's cradle, hopes take seed,
Waiting for morning to gently mend.

The Tapestry of Existence

Each thread entwined, stories unfold,
Colors of life in every seam.
Fates intersect as hearts grow bold,
Woven together in a shared dream.

From the mountains high to oceans wide,
Every stitch holds a memory dear.
In shadows and light, we turn the tide,
Crafting a tale that we hold near.

With hands of hope, we shape our fate,
A mosaic of moments, fragile and grand.
United we sing, we celebrate,
The beauty of lives, together we stand.

Through trials faced, we gather strength,
Embracing the knots that once brought pain.
In the tapestry's breadth, we find our length,
In threads unwoven, we break the chain.

For within the fabric, love endures,
Binding us through thick and thin.
In every tear, a moment pure,
In the tapestry of life, we begin.

Inner Landscapes

In the silence, where thoughts reside,
Vast horizons stretch within the mind.
Mountains of dreams rise high with pride,
Valleys of fears, there we can find.

Each sunrise brings a gentle light,
Illuminating paths that we tread.
Through shadows deep, confronting the night,
In the heart's terrain, courage is fed.

Winds of change caress the soul,
Flowing like rivers, wild and free.
Nature's whispers, a guiding goal,
Mapping the inner topography.

Through forests dense and fields of gold,
We journey inward, seeking truth.
In every scar, a story told,
A testament to our fleeting youth.

For within each heart, a world abides,
Rich with emotions, raw and pure.
In the depths of our being, wisdom hides,
Inner landscapes, forever endure.

The Shelter of the True Self

In whispers soft, the heart will speak,
A haven found, where souls grow meek.
Within these walls, the light shines bright,
Embracing truth, dispelling night.

A gentle breeze, the spirit sways,
In unity, we find our ways.
Each shadow fades, as love comes near,
In silence, we can shed our fear.

The mirror shows a deeper sight,
Reflecting paths to inner light.
With every breath, we mend and heal,
In sacred space, the heart does feel.

Embrace the flaws, the scars we hold,
In stories shared, our truths unfold.
No judgment here, just warmth and grace,
In shelter's arms, we find our place.

Together strong, we rise anew,
In this true self, we are the few.
With open hearts and minds so free,
In shelter's light, we're meant to be.

Awakening the Forgotten Warrior

From ashes deep, the spirit calls,
A brave heart stirs as morning falls.
With every beat, the past ignites,
The warrior wakes, ready to fight.

In shadows cast, the courage grows,
Within the heart, the fire flows.
Not bound by chains of doubt or fear,
The call of purpose now is clear.

With steadfast grip, the sword held high,
To challenge fate, we dare to fly.
In unity, the banners wave,
The hero's path is made to brave.

Through trials faced, the strength is found,
In every scar, a story crowned.
With bold resolve, we claim the day,
The warrior's spirit lights the way.

So rise, dear soul, the time is now,
Embrace your gift, take up the vow.
The forgotten truth shall pave the road,
Within your heart, the warrior glowed.

The Unfolding of Dreams

In quiet nights, the visions stir,
Soft whispers dance, a gentle blur.
Each longing breath, a tale to weave,
In dreamers' hearts, we dare believe.

The canvas waits, with colors bright,
Strokes of hope, in purest light.
With every pulse, the story grows,
A world reborn, as passion flows.

Through winding paths, the visions guide,
With courage strong, we'll turn the tide.
Hand in hand, we chase the gleam,
In unity, we build the dream.

In sacred space, let fears dissolve,
Through trust and love, our dreams evolve.
With open hearts, we take the chance,
In life's great dance, we find our stance.

As dawn breaks forth, the shadows flee,
A brighter world, we're destined to see.
In every step, the promise gleams,
Together we create our dreams.

Clarity from the Chaos

In swirling storms, the mind finds peace,
A tranquil space where thoughts release.
With steady breath, the chaos calms,
In inner stillness, life's sweet psalms.

Through tangled thoughts, we glimpse the truth,
A wiser path, restored in youth.
With open eyes, we seek the light,
In darkness, clarity ignites.

Moments pause, like whispers low,
In silent strength, the heart will grow.
Resilience blooms in subtle grace,
In each small step, we find our place.

With every thought, we shape the day,
Amidst the noise, our spirits play.
In harmony, we learn to trust,
From chaos born, we rise we must.

As dawn awakens, shadows fade,
In clear reflection, dreams are laid.
The journey flows, with every breath,
In clarity, we conquer death.

Chasing Shadows of Truth

In the silence, whispers dwell,
Secrets hidden, tales to tell.
Eyes search wide, yet see so few,
A dance of shadows, chasing true.

The path is winding, never straight,
Each corner turned, we question fate.
In fragments lost, we seek the light,
In shadows woven, truth ignites.

With every step, our hearts all yearn,
For clarity, the soul's return.
Yet in the dark, we learn to fight,
Chasing shadows, craving light.

Beneath the veil of doubt and fear,
We sift through pain to find what's clear.
Through tangled thoughts, we roam and roam,
In search of truth, we find our home.

So let the shadows guide our quest,
For in the chase, we'll learn the best.
With open hearts, we'll face the night,
Chasing shadows, seeking light.

Rebirth from Ashes

In silence deep, the fires burn,
From every loss, we drown, we learn.
The world once bright, now veiled in gray,
Yet from these ashes, hope will play.

With every flame, a story told,
Of courage found and hearts of gold.
The phoenix rises, wings widespread,
Through trials faced, our souls are fed.

In darkness deep, we find our spark,
With every step, we leave a mark.
The strength to stand, we hold so tight,
Rebirth from ashes, into the light.

So let the past drip slowly down,
Like molten gold that wears the crown.
From dust we came, to dust we rise,
In rebirth's dance, we touch the skies.

With every heartbeat, we proclaim,
In this new journey, we're not the same.
Through pain and loss, we boldly lash,
With open arms, we face the crash.

The Heart's Compass

In quiet moments, whispers call,
The heart's compass guides us all.
With intuition, we find our way,
Each gentle nudge, a brand new day.

Through winding paths and shifting sands,
We trust the beat, we hold the strands.
With every choice, the heart expands,
In love's embrace, together we stand.

The storms may rage, the winds may shift,
Yet deep within, our spirits lift.
A tune so sweet, the heart will sing,
In every beat, the hope we bring.

When doubts arise, the compass spins,
Yet through the trials, the journey begins.
With hearts aligned and visions clear,
We'll forge ahead, casting out fear.

So listen close, the heart will share,
The truths we seek, in love and care.
With every pulse, our spirits dance,
The heart's compass leads the chance.

Waking to Wholeness

In gentle dawn, where shadows fade,
Awakening dreams in colors laid.
With open eyes, we start to see,
The magic held in you and me.

As morning breaks, our minds take flight,
In every breath, a spark of light.
The past behind, a brand new choice,
In waking stillness, we find our voice.

With each new day, we shed the skin,
The journey's long, the path begins.
In unity, our hearts embrace,
Waking to wholeness, a sacred space.

Each moment shared, we intertwine,
In every laugh, our souls align.
Together, stronger, through the flow,
In waking wonder, love will grow.

So let the morning be our guide,
With arms wide open, hearts open wide.
Through every rise, we find our way,
Waking to wholeness, day by day.

A Mosaic of Me

Fragments of light, pieces apart,
Colors of dreams, stitched from the heart.
Every scar tells a story anew,
In the tapestry, I find the view.

Moments of laughter, shadows of pain,
Each tiny shard, a link to my chain.
Woven together, a blend so bright,
Creating the canvas of my own light.

Emotions collide, like waves on the shore,
Echoing whispers of what came before.
Shimmering patterns in my own design,
A masterpiece formed with each thought of mine.

In quiet reflection, I piece together,
The fragments of me, bound like a tether.
A mosaic of strength, a blend of grace,
Within every corner, I carve out my space.

Embracing the whole, both dark and the clear,
With each grain of wisdom, I draw myself near.
A mosaic of me, ever changing, free,
In this colorful journey, I choose to be me.

The Road to Reclamation

Each step I take, echoes of the past,
A journey of healing, I hold steadfast.
Cracks in the pavement, a story untold,
Turning the burdens to treasures of gold.

With every sunrise, a brand new chance,
To dance with my shadows, a sacred romance.
The weight of regret lifts with the breeze,
I gather my strength, I'm learning to please.

Paths intertwined, the chaos and calm,
In the heart of the struggle, I find my balm.
Each tear a lesson, each stumble a stride,
Bringing me closer to who's deep inside.

Voices of doubt, they whisper and fade,
For I am the master of dreams I have made.
The road to reclamation, winding and long,
Yet in every twist, I discover my song.

With courage, I walk, unafraid of the night,
Chasing the shadows, embracing the light.
The path may be rough, but I'll never relent,
For this journey is mine, and my heart is content.

Embracing the Unseen

In the whispers of silence, truths come alive,
Between every heartbeat, hidden dreams thrive.
The veil of the ordinary falls gently away,
Revealing the magic that waits in the gray.

Moments unspoken, still water runs deep,
In shadows of longing, my secrets I keep.
The beauty of feelings that often go blind,
Unlocking the depths of the heart and the mind.

A fluttering hope amidst whispers and sighs,
Shimmering sparks beneath untried skies.
Embracing the unseen in each fleeting breath,
In both life and death, eternal in depth.

The dance of the unseen, a delicate thread,
Woven with dreams that have never been said.
A tapestry rich with colors unscanned,
In the canvas of life, I learn to stand.

Finding the glory in what's kept away,
Embracing the hidden in each passing day.
In the shadows of life, treasures be found,
Embracing the unseen, I'm finally unbound.

The Symphony of Self

In the quiet chambers of my core,
Melodies rise, longing for more.
Each note a story, each rest a sigh,
In the symphony of self, I dare to fly.

Harmony dances with a flick of my will,
Creating a resonance, steady and still.
Through crescendos and whispers, I find my way,
In the orchestra of life, I choose to play.

The rhythm of being, a pulse all around,
Echoes of dreams in each heartbeat found.
With every intention, I craft a refrain,
Composing my essence, simple yet plain.

From silence to sound, I embrace the call,
Each heartbeat a drum, together we'll thrall.
The symphony of self, a stunning display,
Resonating truth in a vibrant array.

With colors of life blending notes in the night,
I gather my strength and shine my own light.
In the music of being, I rise and I swell,
For I am the song, the symphony of self.

Treading the Paths Untaken

In twilight's glow, we step with care,
Each choice a whisper in the air.
Footprints fade on the winding way,
We seek the light of a brand new day.

Through thickets dense, the shadows play,
With every turn, we hold our sway.
The heart's compass guides us true,
In search of dreams, we wander through.

Mountains rise, yet we press on,
With every dawn, the night is gone.
Voices call from depths unknown,
In silence found, our courage grown.

Across the vale, where rivers flow,
We find the strength to let love grow.
The unseen paths, they weave and wind,
A journey shared, two hearts aligned.

In every twist, we claim our fate,
For what is lost can still create.
With open hearts, we face the night,
Treading the paths, we chase the light.

Echoes in the Depths

In the cavern's hush, whispers dwell,
Old stories wrapped in a muted spell.
The echoes rise from stony walls,
Each note a memory that softly calls.

Beneath the surface, shadows creep,
Secrets abide in silence deep.
With every step, the past unfolds,
In echoes long, the truth beholds.

Ripples dance in the stillest night,
Faint traces of forgotten light.
Through winding paths that twist and turn,
We seek the flames of wisdom's burn.

The heart resounds with tales of yore,
In depths profound, we long for more.
Time may fade, but voices stay,
In whispers soft that guide our way.

Cloaked in shadows, we journey still,
With every whisper, we find our will.
To understand the depths we tread,
In echoes true, our spirits fed.

The Return to Essence

In stillness found, we pause and breathe,
A journey back, from world we leave.
The essence calls, a gentle nudge,
In quiet moments, we no longer judge.

Through tangled thoughts, the heart can roam,
In simple joys, we carve our home.
A sip of sun, a drop of dew,
Each moment pure, life feels anew.

Beneath the veil of daily strife,
We seek the pulse, the thread of life.
In the rustling leaves, a truth revealed,
The essence shines, our hearts unsealed.

With open arms, we embrace the day,
In every breath, the truth will stay.
To be in touch with what is real,
In the return, we find the feel.

Let go of fear and doubts amassed,
In the essence, hold the steadfast.
With every beat, we find our grace,
In love's embrace, our rightful place.

The Awakening of the Unseen

In the dusk, a soft light glows,
Awakening dreams that time bestows.
Beyond the veil, the whispers rise,
In shadows deep, the truth belies.

A flicker here, a shimmer there,
The unseen world beyond compare.
With open hearts, we seek the dawn,
In every breath, new hopes are drawn.

Through hidden paths, we dare to tread,
In silent wonder, we are led.
The mysteries call, a siren song,
To realms where we know we belong.

Within the stillness, forces play,
As night surrenders to the day.
In dreams reborn, our spirits rise,
Awakening to endless skies.

Embrace the light, let shadows flee,
In the unseen, we find the key.
Awakening hearts, where once was none,
In the vast expanse, we become one.

Journey to the Core

I walk a path of winding light,
With every step, a spark ignites.
Through shadows deep and valleys low,
My spirit soars, as rivers flow.

Mountains rise, they touch the sky,
In silence strong, I learn to fly.
Each breath a song, each beat a door,
Eager heart, to find the core.

The road is long, yet dreams unfold,
In whispered tales, the brave and bold.
With every turn, a lesson shows,
The seed of faith within me grows.

Through storms I march, with steady grace,
In trials faced, I find my place.
No fear can bind, no chain can hold,
This journey deep, a tale retold.

At last I stand, the world in view,
The core revealed, my heart is true.
In unity, the light will beam,
Forever bound, within the dream.

Reflections of the Soul

In pools of stillness, shadows dance,
The essence whispers in a trance.
Mirrors of thought, in silence shine,
Each ripple spreads, a thread divine.

Stories woven, ancient grey,
Through layers deep, they gently sway.
In every glance, a truth unveiled,
In echoes soft, the heart is hailed.

Fulfillment lies in moments shared,
In love's embrace, the soul laid bare.
With gentle hands, we shape the night,
Creating dreams in silver light.

In fleeting time, reflections last,
To shape the future, learn from past.
A dance of light, a tender call,
In sacred space, we rise, we fall.

Through storms of doubt, or winds of grace,
The soul will seek, its rightful place.
In every gaze, a universe spun,
The journey speaks, and we are one.

Whispers in the Wilderness

Beneath the boughs, the secrets sigh,
In gentle winds, the spirits fly.
The trees bear witness, stand so tall,
To silent tales, and nature's call.

Among the ferns, small creatures creep,
In shadows deep, the silence weeps.
The echoes soft, a lover's tune,
Under the gaze of the silver moon.

Each rustle speaks, a language pure,
Of fleeting moments, we endure.
In every path, a choice unfolds,
A story rich, yet untold golds.

The brook's sweet murmur, a calming balm,
It lulls the heart in nature's palm.
With every dawn, the whispers bloom,
In vibrant life, dispelling gloom.

Together here, the wild runs free,
In sacred bonds, you and me.
Let nature's breath our spirits mend,
In wilderness, we find our friend.

Unraveled Threads of Being

In tapestry of dreams, we weave,
The threads of life, what we believe.
With colors bold, and edges frayed,
A tale unfolds, in light and shade.

Each moment stitched, a sacred tie,
In joy and sorrow, we learn to fly.
The fabric's sound, a whisper's grace,
In every knot, we find our place.

From chaos spun, the heart is born,
Through trials faced, we are reborn.
In gentle hands, the threads unwind,
A map of love, in faith we find.

With patience learned, the patterns bloom,
In every stitch, dispelling gloom.
Together weave, our stories blend,
In unity, the threads transcend.

To nurture life, we hold so near,
The art of being, crystal clear.
In every tear, in every thread,
Unraveled truth, we are not led.

Tides of Inner Harmony

In whispers soft, the ocean calls,
A rhythm deep, the heart enthralls.
With every wave, a secret shared,
In silence found, our souls laid bare.

The moon above, a guiding light,
It dances on the sea at night.
In ebb and flow, we learn to trust,
Our spirits rise from ashes, dust.

Each tide that comes, each tide that goes,
Unfolds the truth, the beauty grows.
We sail the currents, bold and free,
In harmony, just you and me.

The calm within, a sacred space,
Where worries fade, and time's embrace.
In unity, the self we find,
As hearts align, and dreams unwind.

With every breath, the waters flow,
A sacred bond, we come to know.
Together strong, through all the strife,
The tides of peace, a cherished life.

The Dance of Authentic Being

In gentle steps, we find our way,
Embracing truth, come what may.
With every twirl, the spirit sings,
Awakening the love it brings.

The light within, it shines so bright,
Illuminates the darkest night.
In every glance, connection stays,
In every heartbeat, love obeys.

We shed the masks, the heavy chains,
Discover strength, as passion reigns.
With open hearts, we leap and bound,
In every moment, joy is found.

Step by step, in sync with grace,
We navigate this timeless space.
In laughter shared, our souls ignite,
The dance of life, pure and bright.

With every spin, our spirits soar,
We celebrate what's at our core.
In vibrant sway, we come alive,
Authentic selves begin to thrive.

A Map of Infinite Paths

Beneath the sky, a myriad of roads,
Each step we take, the story explodes.
In search of dreams, we wander far,
Guided by hope, like a shining star.

The choices made, both big and small,
Shape who we are, if we heed their call.
In winding trails, we twist and turn,
With every lesson, our spirits learn.

From mountain heights to valleys deep,
In every journey, memories keep.
In every fork, a chance to grow,
The unknown paths, where courage flows.

Through shadows cast, we find the light,
In every struggle, we rise in might.
As seasons change, the map unfolds,
In every heart, a story told.

And when we pause to catch our breath,
We see the paths that lead to death.
But life persists in sacred ways,
A map of love that never frays.

Serendipity and Self-Discovery

In random moments, magic waits,
Life's little gifts, it celebrates.
With open hearts, we roam the street,
In every turn, adventures greet.

A chance encounter, a spark ignites,
Turning the mundane into delights.
In laughter shared, connections bloom,
Filling our souls, chasing the gloom.

Through valleys low and mountains high,
In every tear, we learn to fly.
With every stumble, wisdom blooms,
In vibrant colors, life resumes.

Serendipity guides our way,
In every choice, we choose to stay.
In gentle nudges from the heart,
We find the threads that weave our art.

The journey leads us to ourselves,
In hidden corners, love unveils.
We cherish moments, raw and pure,
In self-discovery, we find the cure.

The Harmony of Splintered Notes

In shadows where whispers dwell,
   A melody breaks through,
   Each note a story to tell,
   In fragments, I find you.

   Echoes of laughter ring,
   In the spaces, we collide,
   Together we start to sing,
   In harmony, we abide.

Shattered dreams take their flight,
   Like stars scattered in night,
From chaos, we craft our song,
   In unity, we belong.

With each beat, a soul can rise,
   From silence, the heart learns,
   In brokenness, beauty lies,
   A fire that forever burns.

So let the splinters play free,
A dance of the lost and found,
   In the harmony, we see,
   A love that's unbound.

The Ties that Reconnect

Beneath the strands of time,
Old bonds begin to weave,
Through distance and through rhyme,
In memories, we believe.

A thread that pulls so tight,
Across distances wide,
In darkness, shared light,
With hearts as our guide.

The moments we outgrew,
Still linger in our minds,
A tapestry of you,
In each other, we find.

In laughter, the echoes ring,
A promise, soft but sure,
In whispers, roots take wing,
Forever, we endure.

From scattered paths we roam,
We trace our journey back,
Creating a new home,
On the shared heart's track.

A Pilgrimage to the Real Me

In shadows, paths unfold,
With footsteps worn by dreams,
A journey to be bold,
To mend the broken seams.

Mountains high, valleys low,
With courage, I will climb,
Through storms, I learn to grow,
In rhythm, I find time.

The whispers of the past,
In echo softly call,
With every step steadfast,
I rise, I will not fall.

A mirror shows the truth,
The light within me glows,
In finding my own youth,
The spirit ever flows.

Through every twist and turn,
A flame ignites my soul,
This pilgrimage I yearn,
To make the whole me whole.

The Heart's Schooled Liberation

In chains that once confined,
A heart begins to beat,
With lessons redefined,
Breaking free, bittersweet.

Through pain, the soul is taught,
In silence, strength is found,
With every tear I fought,
A freedom knows no bound.

Each scar a story shares,
In teaching how to love,
The weight of life now bears,
Like wings that lift above.

With whispers of the past,
Resilience in my chest,
In every breath, amassed,
The heart's unending quest.

So here I stand, reborn,
Unfettered by the night,
In the dawn, I am sworn,
To live in the light.

Uniting the Scattered Stars

In the velvet night we gather,
Whispers of dreams on gentle breeze.
Together we shine, no longer lost,
Linked by hope, our hearts at ease.

From distant galaxies we come,
Each flicker tells a tale so bright.
In their glow, forgotten wishes,
Twinkling softly, a guiding light.

Fractured fragments find their way,
Across the vast and endless space.
With every pulse, we intertwine,
Creating beauty, love's embrace.

Our voices rise like shooting stars,
A symphony of souls aligned.
In unity, we break the dark,
In harmony, our fate defined.

Together, scattered stars unite,
A constellation, fierce and bold.
In the night, we weave our dreams,
In every heart, a story told.

Blossoms from the Ashes

From the wreckage life begins,
A tender shoot breaks through the ground.
In shadows deep, where hope once fled,
New blooms emerge, a beauty found.

The flames that scorched, they cleared the path,
To open skies and brighter days.
Resilience wrapped in petals soft,
In vibrant hues, the heart conveys.

Each petal holds a tale of strength,
Of battles fought and tears once shed.
With each new bloom, we rise again,
Transforming hurt to love instead.

Nurtured by the sun's embrace,
We dance beneath the healing rain.
In every garden, life persists,
From ashes, joy will bloom again.

So let the flowers sing of hope,
In every hue, a life renewed.
From broken ground, we will not bow,
We'll thrive despite, embraced by good.

The Altar of Self-Acceptance

In the quiet of the soul's deep trust,
We gather fragments, a sacred space.
Beneath the weight of doubt and shame,
We find our worth, we find our grace.

Each scar a story, each flaw a gift,
In the mirror's gaze, we learn to see.
The beauty lies in being whole,
In loving all that we can be.

With every breath, a choice unfolds,
To honor truths that live within.
We lay our fears upon this stone,
And dance in light, as spirits spin.

Acceptance flows like rivers deep,
Washing away the tales of old.
In vulnerability, strength is found,
In open hearts, a warmth untold.

So here we stand, unmasked and real,
In this sacred space, we will ignite,
The altar where we learn to love,
In every shadow, lies the light.

Reclaiming the Unsung Hero

In the shadows, quietly they tread,
Voices soft, their stories veiled.
Unsung heroes, brave and true,
In every heart, their dreams exhale.

With gentle hands, they shape the world,
In the chaos, they find their way.
Through silent acts of kindness bound,
Their lights will always find the day.

Each small triumph, a hidden gem,
In the fabric of the great unknown.
They rise each time, when hope seems lost,
A quiet strength in seeds they've sown.

So let us lift their voices high,
And weave their tales into the light.
For every hero without a crown,
Deserves to shine and claim their right.

Reclaiming whispers, bold and proud,
In unity, their truth shall soar.
Together now, we'll celebrate,
The unsung heroes we adore.

Pathways to Clarity

In the mist, the road appears,
A journey long through hopes and fears.
With every step, the shadows fade,
Revealing truths that once were made.

The heart beats loud, a guiding drum,
Through tangled paths and distant hums.
Each choice a thread in life's grand weave,
With clarity, we start to believe.

The horizon gleams, a beckoning light,
Illuminating dreams hidden from sight.
With open eyes and open hands,
We grasp the wisdom of life's great plans.

Each moment passed, a lesson learned,
With every twist, new bridges burned.
A clearer path becomes our call,
Embracing rise, accepting fall.

The truth unfolds, a gentle breeze,
Bringing comfort, putting minds at ease.
Through clarity, we find our way,
Emboldened souls, come what may.

Tracing the Lines of Identity

In quiet moments, shadows stir,
Tracing lines where thoughts confer.
A tapestry of all we've been,
In every thread, the light breaks in.

Faces mirror all we've known,
Fleeting time has seeds we've sown.
In laughter shared and tears that fall,
We find our strength within the thrall.

Each story etched upon the skin,
Mapping journeys deep within.
The depths of self, a sacred space,
In every scar, a hint of grace.

Through echoes of what came before,
We forge ahead, we seek for more.
Identity blooms like spring's new rose,
In every petal, the past bestows.

With whispered dreams and starlit skies,
We trace the lines, we see through eyes.
The journey's path is ours to claim,
Embracing all, in love's great name.

The Garden of Self-Realization

In a garden where thoughts take flight,
Seeds of wisdom sprout in light.
Nurtured by hope and inner grace,
Self-realization finds its place.

With every bloom, the past unravels,
In layers deep, the spirit travels.
Pruning doubts, we watch them fall,
Creating space for growth, for all.

Radiant petals of vibrant hue,
Each one a story, each one true.
Through the seasons, we learn to grow,
In this garden, love's rivers flow.

Beneath the sun, we reach for skies,
With open hearts, we live, we rise.
The fragrance sweet, the colors blend,
In self-realization, we comprehend.

In tranquil moments, roots entwine,
A bond so deep, a sacred sign.
In this garden, we become whole,
With every petal, we nourish the soul.

Beneath the Surface: A Revelation

Beneath the waves, the stillness breathes,
A world unseen where mystery weaves.
In the depths, the truth resides,
In whispered currents, fate abides.

Fragments of secrets wait to be found,
In shadows deep, where whispers abound.
A revelation, soft and clear,
Emerging slowly, banishing fear.

Through the depths, our shadows clash,
In the silence, we find a flash.
Of deeper meaning, hidden light,
Illuminating the darkest night.

With every rise, we peel away,
Layers of doubt that led astray.
The ocean's echo sings a song,
Of strength renewed, where we belong.

In depths where fear and courage play,
We surface strong, we find our way.
Beneath the surface, we reveal,
The truths that ultimately heal.

Whispers from the Unspoken

In shadows deep, secrets lie,
Echoes of dreams that never die.
Voices fading, softly speak,
In silence loud, the heart will seek.

Beneath the veil, truths entwine,
In hidden corners, paths align.
Gentle murmurs, a call to dare,
Awakening souls with tender care.

A flicker of hope, a quiet glance,
In every heartbeat, a silent dance.
Bridges built with whispers soft,
Climbing higher, when spirits loft.

The unspoken words we hold dear,
A fragile bond that draws us near.
In every pause, a chance to find,
The beauty woven in the mind.

So listen close, with open heart,
For every silence plays a part.
In whispered tales, the world unfolds,
And in the hush, our truth beholds.

The Reckoning of Resilience

In storms that rage, we stand tall,
With weary hearts, we risk the fall.
Each scar a story, strength confined,
In battles fought, the brave aligned.

Through trials steep, we carve our way,
A flicker of hope in endless gray.
Each stumble learned, each tear a guide,
With every stride, we turn the tide.

The echoes of doubt may haunt our dreams,
Yet through the dark, a light still gleams.
In unity forged, together we rise,
In the depths of struggle, the soul replies.

A tapestry woven with threads of pain,
From ashes we rise, again and again.
With every heartbeat, a fierce decree,
In resilience, we find our key.

So let the winds of change behold,
The stories of strength yet untold.
For in the reckoning, we will find,
The fire of courage that lives behind.

Unmasking the Inner Radiance

Beneath the surface, colors gleam,
A hidden light, a soulful dream.
In shadows cast, the truth may hide,
Yet shining bright, our hearts abide.

With every layer, we peel away,
Unlocking voices, come what may.
The spark within, a blazing flame,
In authenticity, we stake our claim.

When masks are shed, the world can see,
The vibrant dance of you and me.
In vulnerability, strength we find,
Bravely revealing the heart and mind.

The beauty lies in what we share,
In every moment, every dare.
Together we rise, a radiant glow,
Unmasking secrets, letting love flow.

So join the journey, step into light,
Embrace the shadows, ignite the night.
For in the unmasking, we truly grow,
Revealing the radiance we long to show.

Sails of a Sinking Heart

In tempest tossed, the sails unfurl,
As hopes and dreams begin to whirl.
A heart adrift on oceans wide,
In every wave, the tears collide.

Beneath the stars, a guiding light,
In darkest hours, we search for sight.
With every breath, a whisper's plea,
To find the shore, to set us free.

Yet in the depths, a spark remains,
A flicker strong through all the pains.
With every setback, we learn to chart,
The course ahead of a sinking heart.

So hold on tight, through storms and strife,
For every struggle ignites new life.
In sailing forth, we find our path,
Embracing tides, escaping wrath.

Though sails may tear and storms will call,
We'll ride the waves and never fall.
With every heartbeat, we will start,
To dance anew with a sinking heart.

The Inner Odyssey

In the depths of silent dreams,
Whispers from the soul's stream.
Wandering through shadowed halls,
Echoes of my heart's calls.

Each thought a flickering star,
Guiding me both near and far.
Layers peel, the truths unfold,
Stories long forgotten told.

Mirrors show a younger face,
Fleeting moments, time's embrace.
Footsteps tracing ancient ground,
Where my essence can be found.

With every breath, a gentle sigh,
I learn to live, I learn to fly.
Through the turbulence of the mind,
Peace within I seek to find.

Navigating waves of deep despair,
Finding solace in the air.
An inner compass guides the way,
Towards a brighter, hopeful day.

Harmonizing Dissonant Notes

In the clash of chords we meet,
Dissonance beneath our feet.
Voices raised in sharp debate,
Searching for a harmonized fate.

Melodies entwined in strife,
Fractured echoes of our life.
Yet amid the raging sound,
A single note can still be found.

Building bridges with each tone,
Together we can find our own.
Through the chaos, we will strive,
To let our truest selves arrive.

Fingers dancing on the keys,
Crafting peace with gentle ease.
In the symphony we play,
Differences can fade away.

Each dissonant clash, a chance,
To awaken in our dance.
Harmony, the ultimate goal,
Uniting every heart and soul.

Encounters with the Infinite

In the silence of the night,
Stars awaken, softly bright.
They whisper secrets through the void,
Infinite mysteries unalloyed.

Eyes to sky, the cosmos calls,
Galaxies behind the walls.
Time stands still in the embrace,
Of the universe's grace.

Moments blend, a tapestry,
Threads of fate entwined with me.
Every heartbeat, a spark ignites,
Illuminating endless heights.

Through the portals of the mind,
Connections vast, the truth I'm blind.
Yet in this dance of time and space,
I find belonging, I find my place.

Encounters with the great unknown,
In every breath, I'm not alone.
Infinity, a guide so wise,
Reflecting in my searching eyes.

The Sanctuary Within

Nestled deep, a sacred space,
Where my spirit finds its grace.
Walls of calm, a tranquil sea,
A haven crafted just for me.

In stillness, shadows softly fade,
Stitched with love, a gentle braid.
Each thought, a flower in bloom,
Filling the heart, dispelling gloom.

Here, the noise of life grows dim,
A whispered prayer, a quiet hymn.
Embracing all that I have been,
The light inside me shines within.

The world outside may spin and sway,
Yet in this peace, I choose to stay.
Terracotta, worn and raw,
Finding strength in my own law.

United with the breath of time,
Rhythms pulse, a sacred rhyme.
In this sanctuary, I belong,
A refuge where I feel so strong.

Whispers of the Radiant Heart

In shadows cast by gentle light,
A heartbeat secrets, soft and bright.
Amid the quiet, dreams take flight,
Whispers dance in the still of night.

Love's embrace, a tender song,
Guiding souls where they belong.
In every hush, where hearts grow strong,
A radiant warmth that feels so wrong.

Beneath the surface, trust reveals,
A pulse that time so deftly steals.
With every breath, the spirit heals,
In the silence, love conceals.

Unspoken truths in every glance,
A flicker, a spark, a sweet romance.
Embrace the pause, the shared expanse,
In whispers soft, we find our chance.

Hold tight the moments, fleeting, rare,
For in each whisper, memories flare.
The radiant heart, our souls laid bare,
Together in love, beyond compare.

The Mirror's Secret

In glass reflections, truths reside,
A thousand worlds where secrets hide.
With each facade, we turn the tide,
In silent stares, our dreams abide.

Beneath the surface, shadows creep,
In quiet depths, the heart can't sleep.
A mirror's gaze, a promise steep,
In every crack, our sorrows heap.

Yet in the shards, a light breaks through,
A kaleidoscope of colors true.
In fractured forms, we start anew,
Finding strength in what we view.

Reflections dance, a timeless game,
Unveiling soft, unspoken name.
In every glance, we're not the same,
The mirror knows, and we feel shame.

But in acceptance, we find peace,
Each flaw embraced, a sweet release.
In honesty, our hearts increase,
The mirror whispers: love does cease.

Yet every flaw a bridge to cross,
In every judgment, find the gloss.
With heart aligned, we bear the loss,
The mirror's secret, love's embossed.

Eclipsing Doubt

When shadows loom and thoughts obscure,
A flicker of faith, our hearts ensure.
In moments dark, we seek the pure,
Eclipsing doubt, we find the cure.

A whisper calls in quiet spaces,
Illuminating all the traces.
With every step, our spirit races,
To overcome what fear embraces.

Through trials faced, we rise again,
In strength of unity, peace we gain.
With open hearts, we shed the strain,
Eclipsing doubt, we break the chain.

When storms arise, we stand as one,
Beneath the clouds, we find the sun.
In whispered hopes, our battle's won,
Together, we've just begun.

In every moment, courage breeds,
For love, we plant our steadfast seeds.
With faith as root, it gently leads,
Eclipsing doubt, our spirit feeds.

So hold the light when shadows fall,
In radiant grace, we heed the call.
With every challenge, we stand tall,
Eclipsing doubt, we conquer all.

The Fabric of Authenticity

Woven threads of truth and care,
In every heart, a tale to share.
Unraveled fears, yet bold we dare,
In fabric textured, love lays bare.

From every stitch, a voice rings clear,
In vibrant hues, our dreams appear.
Together strong, we persevere,
The fabric spun from hope and cheer.

In honest hearts, authenticity,
We find our place, our unity.
In every tear, a tapestry,
A shared embrace, our symphony.

Through storms of doubt, we weave our tale,
In threads of gold, we shall not fail.
With hearts ablaze, we set our sail,
Navigating truth, we will prevail.

So wear your truth like finest cloth,
In vibrant colors, no longer sloth.
In every moment, showcase growth,
The fabric of authenticity, our troth.

In unity, our stories flow,
A canvas rich, where dreams will grow.
In every heart, let courage glow,
The fabric binding us, we know.

Connected Threads of Existence

In the web of life we weave,
Each thread holds a tale to tell.
Intertwined by hopes and dreams,
Together, we flourish and swell.

In shadows we find the light,
A bond that never shall break.
Through storms and gentle nights,
With love, our hearts awake.

Each encounter, a stitch so bold,
Time's loom can never fray.
Colors bright and stories old,
Connected, come what may.

In whispers of the gentle breeze,
Threads carry whispers of the past.
In weaving, we find our peace,
A legacy made to last.

So embrace the ties we have,
For unity holds the key.
In this beautiful tapestry,
We are one, you and me.

Navigating the Inner Ocean

A sea of thoughts deep and wide,
Currents pull, then push and sway.
In silence, we learn to glide,
Chasing fears that drift away.

With every wave, the tides shall shift,
A journey through the ebb and flow.
We search for treasures, truth a gift,
In the depths where dreams still glow.

Some storms may roar, some calm may reign,
Yet through it all we stand firm.
Amid the joy and the pain,
We're sailors, hearts eager to learn.

Beneath the surface, shadows dance,
Finding light in hidden caves.
In each moment, there's a chance,
To ride the waves, to be brave.

With stars to guide, we chart our way,
Through waters dark, through skies so bright.
Navigating this vast array,
We discover our inner light.

The Portraits We Paint

Each brushstroke tells a story true,
Colors blend, emotions flow.
In canvas blank, dreams are imbued,
A world created; we bestow.

With hues of joy and shades of sorrow,
We capture moments, fleeting and rare.
Each piece, a glimpse of tomorrow,
In the gallery of life we share.

Figures dance upon the page,
Narratives form, voices arise.
In every palette, love, and rage,
Reflections of the heart, the skies.

Portraits invite us to connect,
To see the beauty in our flaws.
In art, we find the perfect effect,
The language beyond mere applause.

So paint your truth, don't hesitate,
In vibrant strokes, let courage beam.
In this shared canvas, we create,
A world alive, a living dream.

The Garden of Embers

In the dusk, where shadows play,
A garden thrives, aglow with heat.
From ashes rise, what once gave way,
New life blossoms, bittersweet.

With petals bright, a fierce intent,
In every spark, the stories grow.
From charred remains, our hearts are spent,
In the soil, love's seeds we sow.

The fire's dance, a sacred rite,
Illuminates the darkest soil.
In every ember, hope ignites,
A reminder through the toil.

The night's embrace, a tender shroud,
While stars above our dreams align.
In silence, we stand fierce and proud,
The garden waits, with love divine.

So tend to the flames that guide your way,
In the garden, let your heart wander.
For even in night, there's a brand new day,
In the glow, we grow ever fonder.

Milton Keynes UK
Ingram Content Group UK Ltd.
UKHW020037271124
451585UK00012B/909